Hopkinsville-Christian County Public Library

MAY -- 2021

# Philadelphia 76ERS

BY JIM GIGLIOTTI

Published by The Child's World®
1980 Lookout Drive • Mankato, MN 56003-1705
800-599-READ • www.childsworld.com

Cover: © Joe Robbins.
Photographs ©: AP Images: 22; Nick Wass 5, 26; Paul Shane 9; Chris Szagola 12; George Wildman 17; Matt Slocum 26 (2); Michael Dwyer 26. Dreamstime.com: Dave Newman 13. Newscom: Kyle Ross/Icon SW 6, 10; Steven Falk/TNS 18, Steven Dowell/TNS 25; Harry Walker/KRT 29.

Copyright © 2020 by The Child's World®
All rights reserved. No part of this book may be reproduced or utilized in any form or by any means without written permission from the publisher.

ISBN 9781503824485
LCCN 2018964293

Printed in the United States of America
PA02416

## ABOUT THE AUTHOR

Jim Gigliotti has worked for the University of Southern California's athletic department, the Los Angeles Dodgers, and the National Football League. He is now an author who has written more than 100 books, mostly for young readers, on a variety of topics.

# TABLE OF CONTENTS

Go, 76ers! . . . . . . . . . . . . . . . . . . . . . . . . . . . . . 4
Who Are the 76ers? . . . . . . . . . . . . . . . . . . . . 7
Where They Came From . . . . . . . . . . . . . . . . 8
Who They Play . . . . . . . . . . . . . . . . . . . . . . . 11
Where They Play . . . . . . . . . . . . . . . . . . . . . 12
The Basketball Court . . . . . . . . . . . . . . . . . 15
Good Times . . . . . . . . . . . . . . . . . . . . . . . . . 16
Tough Times . . . . . . . . . . . . . . . . . . . . . . . . 19
All the Right Moves . . . . . . . . . . . . . . . . . . 20
Heroes Then . . . . . . . . . . . . . . . . . . . . . . . . 23
Heroes Now . . . . . . . . . . . . . . . . . . . . . . . . 24
What They Wear . . . . . . . . . . . . . . . . . . . . . 27

    Team Stats . . . . . . . . . . . . . . . . . . . . 28
    Glossary . . . . . . . . . . . . . . . . . . . . . . 30
    Find Out More . . . . . . . . . . . . . . . . . 31
    Index . . . . . . . . . . . . . . . . . . . . . . . . . 32

# GO, 76ERS!

Some of the NBA's all-time superstars have played for the 76ers. Wilt Chamberlain, Julius Erving, and Allen Iverson are just a few of them. In 2019, young **center** Joel Embiid led the team to the playoffs. It was the 76ers' first time in six seasons. Is Embiid the next player in the long line of team greats? The 76ers and their fans sure think so.

Big Ben Simmons is another part of a new wave of great young 76ers players.

5

Ben Simmons looks to make a pass as he and the Sixers play an Atlantic Division rival, the New York Knicks.

# WHO ARE THE 76ERS?

The 76ers play in the Atlantic Division. That division is part of the NBA's Eastern Conference. The other teams in the Atlantic Division are the Boston Celtics, the Brooklyn Nets, the New York Knicks, and the Toronto Raptors. The 76ers last won the division in the 2001 season. However, they have made the **playoffs** eight times since then.

# WHERE THEY CAME FROM

The 76ers played in the first NBA season in 1950. Then, the team was called the Syracuse Nationals. The team moved to Philadelphia in the 1964 season. It became known as the 76ers. Often, the team is called the Sixers. A "76er" refers to 1776. That was the year the United States was born. The team's **logo** includes 13 stars. There were 13 states in the US in 1776.

Darryl Dawkins was so powerful that he twice broke the backboard making a dunk.

9

To reach the top of the Eastern Conference, the Sixers have to overcome the Boston Celtics.

10

# WHO THEY PLAY

The 76ers play 82 games each season. They play 41 games at home and 41 on the road. They play four games against the other Atlantic Division teams. They play 36 games against other Eastern Conference teams. Finally, the Sixers play each of the teams in the Western Conference twice. That's a lot of basketball! In June, the winners of the Western and Eastern Conference play each other in the NBA Finals.

# WHERE THEY PLAY

The 76ers play their home games at the Wells Fargo Center. The **arena** opened for the 1997 season. The Philadelphia Flyers pro hockey team also plays there. The Sixers' title banners hang from the rafters. Banners with the names Bruce Springsteen and Billy Joel do, too. Those famous musicians have played sold-out concerts at the arena.

A bank sponsors the 76ers home court. Franklin the Dog is the team's mascot (left). He was named for Ben Franklin, the Founding Father from Philadelphia.

13

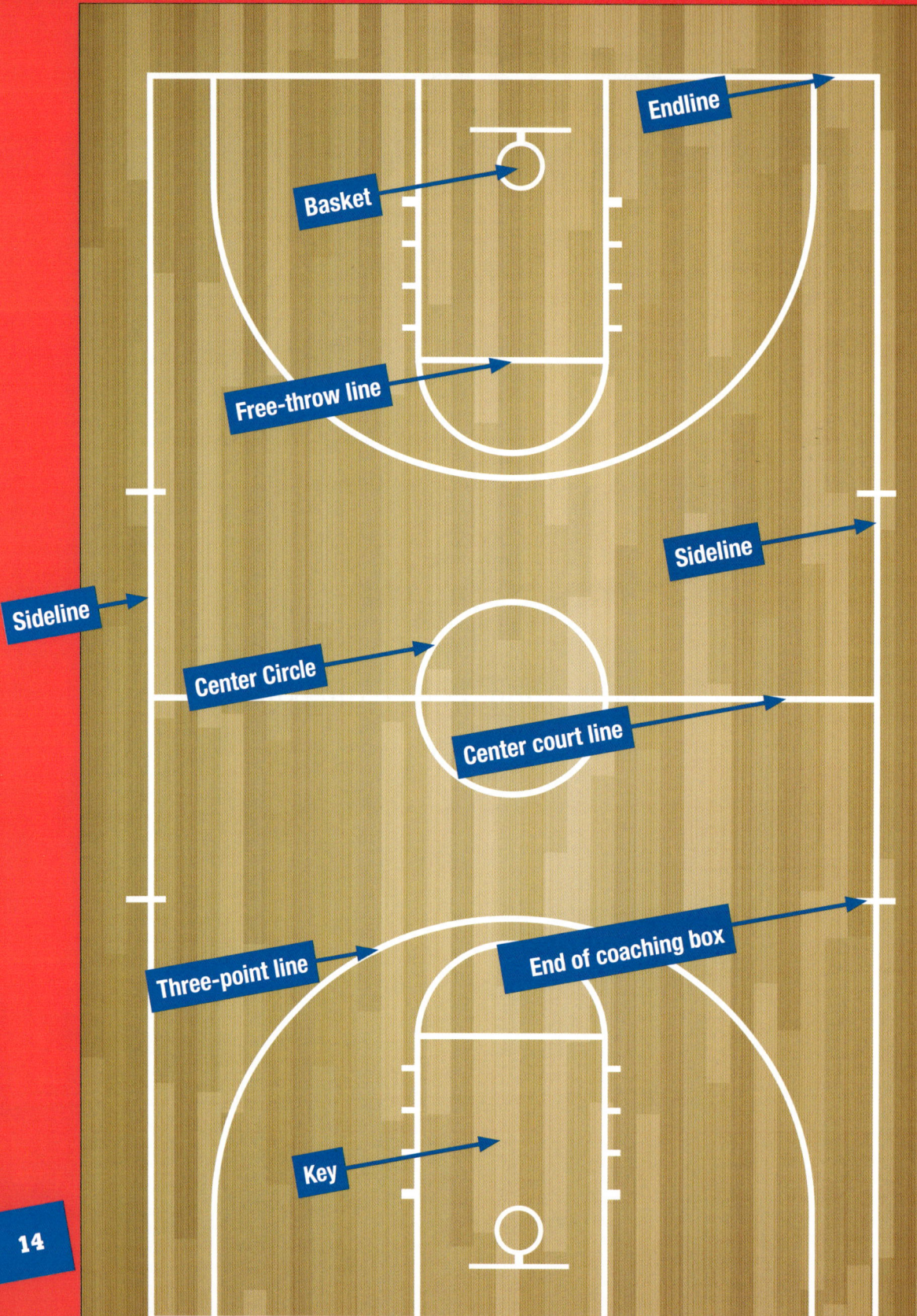

# THE BASKETBALL COURT

An NBA court is 94 feet long and 50 feet wide (28.6 m by 15.24 m). Nearly all the courts are made from hard maple wood. Rubber mats under the wood help make the floor springy. Each team paints the court with its logo and colors. Lines on the court show the players where to take shots. The diagram on the left shows the important parts of the NBA court.

The 2002 NBA All-Star Game was played at the 76ers' home arena.

# GOOD TIMES

The Sixers were really good for a very long time. The team made the playoffs in each of its first 22 seasons. The team won two league titles in that time—1955 and 1967. The 1980s were a great time for the 76ers. They won the NBA title in 1983, and they made the playoffs every season except 1987–88. After some down years, the team roared back in 2018. The Sixers won 52 games that season.

Philadelphia's Moses Malone fought with the Lakers' Kareem Abdul-Jabbar in the 1983 NBA Finals.

Getting dunked on by stars like Anthony Davis of the Pelicans was nothing new for Philadelphia in a tough 2016 season.

18

# TOUGH TIMES

The Sixers have not been bad very often. But when they have been bad, they have been awful! In 2016, the 76ers lost their first 18 games. It didn't get much better after that. The team finished with only 10 wins. Only one other team in NBA history won fewer games in a full season. Unfortunately, that was a Sixers team, too. Philadelphia was 9–73 in 1973.

# ALL THE RIGHT MOVES

Julius Erving soared through the air like no one else. "Dr. J" could take off from the free-throw line and dunk a basketball! Darryl Dawkins was also known for powerful dunks. Current big man Joel Embiid can dunk with the best of them, too. Embiid's top moves are because of his quick feet. His amazing footwork came from playing soccer as a kid. He grew up in Cameroon, a country in Africa.

In basketball, a "big man" means, of course, a player who is tall and strong. It can also refer to a team's best player.

Few players have ever soared so high or dunked so well as the great Julius "Dr. J" Erving.

Wilt "The Stilt" Chamberlain was one of the NBA's best all-around stars.

# HEROES THEN

Hall of Famer Dolph Schayes was the team's first star. Center Wilt Chamberlain was a powerful scorer and rebounder. Julius Erving could do just about anything with the basketball. Billy Cunningham helped the Sixers win the league title in 1968 as a player. Then he coached the team to the championship in 1983. Allen Iverson was an All-Star eight years in a row for the 76ers in the 2000s.

# HEROES NOW

Joel Embiid is the Sixers' top player. He is a seven-foot (2.1-m) center. But he can move like a **point guard**. The Sixers made a big trade to get Jimmy Butler in the 2018–19 season. His nickname is "Jimmy Buckets." He's not all about scoring baskets, though. He's great on defense, too. Another big star is Ben Simmons. He scores, rebounds, dishes out **assists**, and steals the ball.

Jimmy Butler joined the 76ers in 2019. His veteran leadership will help the team's young stars improve.

25

# 76ers Uniforms

# WHAT THEY WEAR

NBA players wear a **tank top** jersey. Players wear team shorts. Each player can choose his own sneakers. Some players also wear knee pads or wrist guards.

Each NBA team has more than one jersey style. The pictures at left show some of the 76ers' jerseys.

The NBA basketball is 29.5 inches (75 cm) around. It is covered with leather. The leather has small bumps called pebbles.

The pebbles on a basketball help players grip it.

# TEAM STATS

Here are some of the all-time career records for the Philadelphia 76ers. These stats are complete through all of the 2018–19 NBA regular season.

| GAMES | |
|---|---|
| Hal Greer | 1,122 |
| Dolph Schayes | 996 |

| POINTS PER GAME | |
|---|---|
| Wilt Chamberlain | 27.62 |
| Allen Iverson | 27.61 |

| ASSISTS PER GAME | |
|---|---|
| Ben Simmons | 7.9 |
| Maurice Cheeks | 7.3 |

| REBOUNDS PER GAME | |
|---|---|
| Wilt Chamberlain | 23.9 |
| Dolph Schayes | 12.1 |

| STEALS PER GAME | |
|---|---|
| Allen Iverson | 2.27 |
| Maurice Cheeks | 2.27 |

| FREE-THROW PCT. | |
|---|---|
| J.J. Redick | .898 |
| Jodie Meeks | .886 |

**ALLEN IVERSON**

### THREE-POINT FIELD GOALS

| | |
|---|---|
| Allen Iverson | 885 |
| Robert Covington | 707 |

# GLOSSARY

**arena** *(uh-REE-nuh)* the building in which a basketball team plays its games

**assists** *(uh-SISTS)* passes that lead directly to a basket

**center** *(SEN-ter)* a basketball position that plays near the basket

**logo** *(LOW-go)* a team or company's symbol

**playoffs** *(PLAY-offs)* games played between top teams to determine who moves ahead

**point guard** *(POYNT GARD)* a basketball player who most often dribbles and passes the ball

**tank top** *(TANK TOP)* a style of shirt that has straps over the shoulders and no sleeves

# FIND OUT MORE

### IN THE LIBRARY

DeMocker, Michael. *Joel Embiid*. Kennett Square, PA: Purple Toad Publishing, 2018.

Schaller, Bob with Coach Dave Harnish. *The Everything Kids' Basketball Book (3rd Edition).* Avon, MA: Adams Media, 2017.

Whiting, Jim. *The Philadelphia 76ers (The NBA: A History of Hoops).* Mankato, MN: Creative Paperbacks, 2017.

### ON THE WEB

Visit our website for links about the Philadelphia 76ers:
**childsworld.com/links**

Note to Parents, Teachers, and Librarians: We routinely verify our Web links to make sure they are safe and active sites. So encourage your readers to check them out!

Abdul-Jabbar, Kareem, 17
Africa, 20
Atlantic Division, 7, 11
Boston Celtics, 7, 10
Brooklyn Nets, 7
Butler, Jimmy, 24, 25
Chamberlain, Wilt, 4, 22, 23
court, 15
Cunningham, Billy, 23
Davis, Anthony, 18
Dawkins, Darryl, 9, 20
Eastern Conference, 7
Embiid, Joel, 4, 20, 24
Erving, Julius, 4, 20, 21, 23

Franklin, 13
Iverson, Allen, 4, 23
jerseys, 27
Joel, Billy, 12
Malone, Moses, 17
New York Knicks, 7
Philadelphia Flyers, 12
Schayes, Dolph, 23
Simmons, Ben, 5, 6, 24
Springsteen, Bruce, 12
Syracuse Nationals, 8
Toronto Raptors, 7
Wells Fargo Center, 12
Western Conference, 11